how do plants survive?

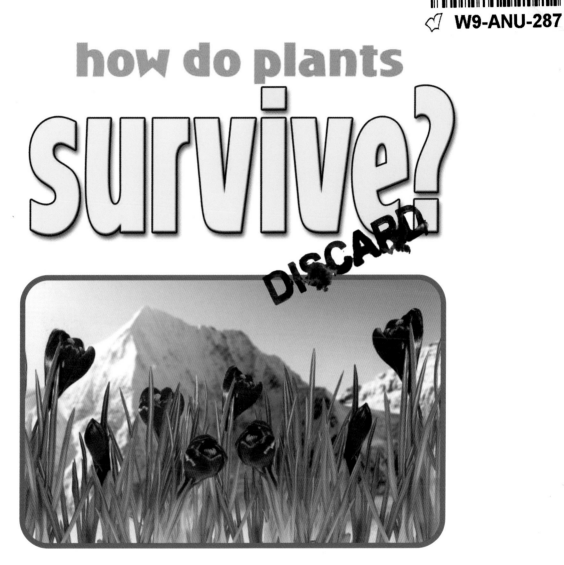

by Kelley MacAulay

🍂 **Crabtree Publishing Company**

www.crabtreebooks.com

Plants Close-Up

Author
Kelley MacAulay

Publishing plan research and development
Reagan Miller, Crabtree Publishing Company

Editorial director
Kathy Middleton

Editors
Reagan Miller, Crystal Sikkens

Proofreader
Kelly McNiven

Notes to adults
Reagan Miller

Photo research
Crystal Sikkens

Design
Ken Wright

**Production coordinator
and prepress technician**
Ken Wright

Print coordinator
Margaret Amy Salter

Photographs
Shutterstock: cover, pages 1, 3, 5, 6, 7, 8, 9, 10, 11, 13,
    14, 15, 16, 18, 20, 22, 23, 24 (except grasslands)
Thinkstock: pages 4, 17, 19, 21, 24 (grasslands)
Wikimedia Commons: Alastair Rae: page 12

Library and Archives Canada Cataloguing in Publication

MacAulay, Kelley, author
    How do plants survive? / Kelley MacAulay.

(Plants close-up)
Includes index.
Issued in print and electronic formats.
ISBN 978-0-7787-1285-5 (bound).--ISBN 978-0-7787-0003-6 (pbk.).--
ISBN 978-1-4271-9367-4 (html).--ISBN 978-1-4271-9371-1 (pdf)

    1. Plant ecophysiology--Juvenile literature. 2. Plants--Habitat--
Juvenile literature. I. Title. II. Series: Plants close-up

QK717.M23 2013   j581.7   C2013-904030-7
                                        C2013-904031-5

Library of Congress Cataloging-in-Publication Data

MacAulay, Kelley.
  How do plants survive? / Kelley Macaulay.
    p. cm. -- (Plants close-up)
  Includes an index.
  ISBN 978-0-7787-1285-5 (reinforced library binding) -- ISBN 978-0-7787-0003-6
(pbk.) -- ISBN 978-1-4271-9371-1 (electronic pdf) -- ISBN 978-1-4271-9367-4
(electronic html)
  1. Plants--Juvenile literature. 2. Plants--Habitat--Juvenile literature. I. Title.
II. Series: Plants close-up.

QK49.M174 2013
580--dc23
                                        2013023433

Crabtree Publishing Company

Printed in Hong Kong/092013/BK20130703

www.crabtreebooks.com   1-800-387-7650

**Published in Canada
Crabtree Publishing**
616 Welland Ave.
St. Catharines, Ontario
L2M 5V6

**Published in the United States
Crabtree Publishing**
PMB 59051
350 Fifth Avenue, 59th Floor
New York, New York 10118

**Published in the United Kingdom
Crabtree Publishing**
Maritime House
Basin Road North, Hove
BN41 1WR

**Published in Australia
Crabtree Publishing**
3 Charles Street
Coburg North
VIC 3058

Contents

Plants are alive!

Plants are living things. All plants need air, sunlight, and water to stay alive.

Each part of a plant does a job to help it stay alive and grow.

A job to do

A plant's roots
take in water from
the soil. The roots
hold the plant in
the ground. The
plant's stem
brings water and
food to other
parts of the plant.
It can also store
food and water.

stem

soil

roots

A plant's leaves make food using sunlight, air, and water. Seeds grow in flowers and fruits. Seeds become new plants.

leaves

seeds

kiwi fruit

Staying alive

A **habitat** is the natural place where an animal or a plant lives. Animals and plants live in habitats where they can get the things they need to survive. Animals can move around to find food, water, and shelter.

Plants cannot move around to find food or water. They must survive in the place where they are growing. Different plants use their parts in different ways to help them survive and grow in their habitats.

Dry deserts

Cacti are **desert** plants. Deserts are hot, sandy places with little rain. Cacti have long, **shallow** roots. Shallow roots are not deep underground. They soak up a lot of water when it rains.

cacti

Cacti also have thick waxy stems that hold in water. They store the water in their stems to use when there is no rain. A round barrel cactus can store a lot of water.

In the tundra

The **tundra** is land at the top of Earth near the North Pole. It is very cold with strong winds. Tundra plants, such as this purple saxifrage, must stay out of cold winds. They grow low to the ground and close together.

Some tundra plants have fuzzy hairs on their stems and leaves to protect them from the cold.

Hot forests

Rain forests are hot places. There is a lot of sunlight in these forests, but it also rains almost every day. The sunlight and rain make it easy for many trees to grow tall.

Tall trees in rain forests block sunlight from reaching the forest floor. **Vines** are plants that can climb. They attach to trees and climb up them to reach the sunlight.

vines

Four seasons

In some places, trees change as the seasons change. Spring and summer are warm, sunny seasons. Trees grow many leaves and make a lot of food. The trees store some of the food for colder weather.

Autumn and winter are colder seasons. There is less sunlight. Leaves cannot make food. They change color and fall to the ground. The trees use their stored food to stay alive until spring.

Underwater plants

Some plants can grow under water. Underwater plants grow in shallow water. Shallow water is not very deep. Sunlight can shine through shallow water to the plants. Some animals, such as manatees, eat the plants.

kelp

Kelp are plants that grow in oceans near the shore. Kelp attach to rocks on the ocean floor. They have long stems that reach sunlight near the water's surface.

Wetland plants

In a **wetland** the land is covered with water. Water lilies grow in wetlands. They have long **stalks** that hold their leaves and flowers above the water. The stalks grow from a stem buried in the mud below.

water lily

stalk

Mangrove trees also grow in wetlands. Parts of their roots grow up out of the water. The wide roots keep the trees from falling over. The roots also take in air.

Open grasslands

Grasslands are open, flat areas of land. Strong winds blow across grasslands. Grasses in grasslands have long roots growing deep in the ground. The long roots hold the grasses in place.

Baobab trees grow in hot, dry grasslands. They only grow leaves when there is water. When it is dry, the trees survive using stored water in their large trunks, or stems.

trunk

Words to know

desert 10–11 **grassland** 22–23 **habitat** 8, 9 **shallow** 10, 18

stalk 20 **tundra** 12–13 **vines** 15 **wetland** 20–21

Notes for adults and an activity

Invite readers to share what they learned about the ways plants survive in different habitats. Ask the following questions to prompt discussion and assess understanding:

• What do plants need to stay alive and grow? (Air, sunlight, and water)

• How do some tundra plants protect themselves from the cold? (Some tundra plants have fuzzy hairs on their stems and leaves.)

• How do grasses growing in grasslands survive the strong winds? (These grasses have long, deep roots to hold them in place.)

• Ask children to consider how their lives would change if they suddenly found themselves living in a different habitat, such as a desert, a rainforest, even the tundra! How would they get food, water, and shelter? Brainstorm ideas and have children draw a picture and write a paragraph identifying how they would survive in their new habitat.

Learning more

Books

Plants in Different Habitats (Nature's Changes) by Bobbie Kalman. Crabtree Publishing Company (2006)

Amazing Plants (Amazing Science) by Sally Hewitt. Crabtree Publishing Company (2008)

Websites

The Great Plant Escape: Children team up with Detective LePlant to explore how a plant grows.
  http://urbanext.illinois.edu/gpe/index.cfm

Plant Adaptations: This animated video expands on the concept of plant adaptations.
  http://studyjams.scholastic.com/studyjams/jams/science/
    plants/plant-adaptations.htm